How to Get Out of Debt

The Science of Living

Kostadin Ristovski

Mendon Cottage Books

JD-Biz Publishing

Disclaimer

The information is this book is provided for informational purposes only. It is not intended to be used and medical advice or a substitute for proper medical treatment by a qualified health care provider. The information is believed to be accurate as presented based on research by the author.

The contents have not been evaluated by the U.S. Food and Drug Administration or any other Government or Health Organization and the contents in this book are not to be used to treat cure or prevent disease.

The author or publisher is not responsible for the use or safety of any diet, procedure or treatment mentioned in this book. The author or publisher is not responsible for errors or omissions that may exist.

Warning

The Book is for informational purposes only and before taking on any diet, treatment or medical procedure, it is recommended to consult with your primary health care provider.

Our books are available at
1. Amazon.com
2. Barnes and Noble
3. Itunes
4. Kobo
5. Smashwords
6. Google Play Books

Table of Contents

Introduction

Debt is a word that everyone is afraid of. Nobody likes this word, not even banks. Banks like it when others are in debt to them. Anyway, if you are in debt, it is not the end of the world. It only means that you are in a bad financial position and that is something that you need to change. If we take a look at the debt statistics, over 70% of the students in USA are in debt with average sum of $30.000 per student. Now this is a huge percent and very high sum of money. Part of the students will struggle for a very, very long time to get out of debt and have a life with financial freedom. But some of them will do it much quicker, much easier. *Why? Why some students get out of debt faster than others? Why some people are more afraid of debt than others?* These are some of the questions that you can expect to find answers to in the next couple of pages.

Every single person is different and unique. Every person has different skills, advantages and weaknesses that they develop over time. A lot of people spent years researching, trying to find a formula on how to become financially free that will work on everyone, but they couldn't find it. Because, I am going to mention it again, everyone is different and unique. This was the main reason why they failed. They thought that only because something worked out for someone, it will work for someone else as-well. Or, only because something did not work out for someone, it will not work out for someone else. Do not expect to find the secret formula on how to get out of debt in this book, because it is not here. It is not out of the book, it does not exist. The only formula that works for you is inside you. This part of the book will help you find out how you can get the best out of yourself and how to create this formula that will help you get out of debt.

Getting out of debt will make you much, much stronger. Yes, you will be disappointed while you are in debt and maybe mad at yourself and others, but you will also manage to build a stronger character. Being in debt, and then getting out of it will make you much, much stronger. Your patience will increase, your discipline will improve, you will build endurance and most important of all, you will have more courage. Why? Well, you can say "I had debt, but I won and now I am financially free." This is something that all-time debt-free people cannot say.

There is another part of this topic that is worth mentioning. Almost all of the successful and rich entrepreneurs had debt. Not before they started their business, but while they had it. Most of them started in garages, with some or no money. They borrowed money from friends and family, but **they believed in themselves**. They had the courage and they knew their advantages and disadvantages, their strengths and their weaknesses. And again, they had patience. They did not become rich overnight, but they knew that they are on the right track and they kept going. This is the main reason why some students get out of debt faster than others, because they **know** themselves. They are aware of their skills, their weaknesses, their strengths, expertise, and they know their value. These people use the information they have to earn money and afford a better life.

Bill Gates said "If you are born poor, it's not your mistake. But if you die poor, it's your mistake." At the beginning of your life, you know nothing about the world nor about yourself. As you grow, you increase your value as person. And that's all that changes right? You become more educated, you absorb knowledge, you become more experienced in certain area and that's it. What you do from the moment you are born, till you die is what builds you as a person. Why it is your fault if you die poor? Because you spent the time between on something not worth doing. Today, we live in an age dominated by technology. There are thousands of people using the internet for the right purpose, but so many more wasting their time playing useless games online or reading stuff that are not important. In the 21st century we all have almost the same recourses. But there is one recourse that we cannot control and that is time. No matter what we do, it goes on. So, if you want to increase your value as a person, if you want to put your personality and skills to work and start earning the money you truly deserve, then you need to get the most out of your limited time. And in order to do that, you need to make a schedule and plan, that's what the last chapter of this short book is about.

Let's talk a bit more about being debt-free. How does it feel being debt-free? This is something a lot of people imagine. But what they imagine is a much easier life with less stressful decisions, a life with less time spent on planning the budget about the next day, week or month and a life that allows you to sleep well at night. In fact, none of this is true. Let's start from the beginning. Less stressful decisions? Not really. Life does not care about our money. We face challenges and problems every day. Yes, some of the problems can be solved with money, but not all. The life of a person does not depend on the current financial position. It depends on the way a person thinks. Let's continue and say couple of words about planning. Budget planning is again, something that does not depend on how much money or debt you currently have. If a person knows the real value of planning his time and his budget, he will do it regardless of his financial position.

Now, let's start discussing about creating the "secret" formula for you. The reason why you are reading this book is probably because you are in debt or you want to improve your financial position. The reason why some people are in debt while others is because the ones in debt spend more than the amount they earn. On the other hand, the financial free or as some people call them rich, earn a lot more than they spend. But this is not something that you didn't know until now, right? This is something that every single person knows. But this is very important! You can see that the two parts of the equation that define your financial positions are the money you earn and the money you spend. Now, this is again something that you knew, but let's keep digging in these two categories. These two categories will be the next two chapters of this book.

Earning money

In order to get out of debt you need to pay off the amount you owe. Now, in order to pay that amount, you need to earn the money.

This book does not support/encourage earning money illegal ways.

Today there are a lot of different jobs that allow you to earn money. First of all, I am going to focus on the types of jobs.

In most countries, the less paid jobs are the ones that require a lot of physical work and less mental work. (Example: People that work in fast-food stands such as McDonalds, workers, farmers, cleaners and so on.) It is not that these people have an easy job, but because it can be done by almost anyone! **The salary is created based on the demand and the supply for the job position.** All of the professions that I mentioned in brackets can be done without any formal education, without any specific knowledge. Yes, it might need some short practice in order to gain experience, but it is nothing compared to a lot of other professions.

Now, we will not focus on the demand, because that is not where you are. You are focused on earning money in order to earn enough to get out of debt and improve your financial position. In order to do that, you need to take a look at the supply part and make sure you offer something valuable. The supply are the real people, they are the ones applying for these positions. Now, why people apply to some jobs and not to all. Probably because they do not have enough knowledge and experience in all areas. However, there is something else as-well.

Different jobs have different responsibilities. A manager has a lot more responsibility than the person under him in the hierarchy. The teacher has more responsibility than the person cleaning the school.

Different jobs have different environment. Some people prefer one environment over another one. Some people prefer working in a quiet environment, some prefer working in a clear environment. Some people don't really pay attention to the environment.

Different jobs have different colleagues and managers. Some jobs require a lot more communication and reporting to the manager and some people are not comfortable doing that.

Different jobs have different amount of risk. It is different to work as a cleaner and as a miner.

The more difficult the job is, the more responsibility it has, the worse environment it has and the more risky it is, the bigger the salary is.

Doctors have huge salary, because their responsibility is on a very high level and the environment is changing depends on the patients. Managers have high salary, because of their responsibility. Miners have high salary, because of the risk that the job has.

All of these are reasons why some people want to work one job and dislike another one. Now, I am not telling you that you should do everything in order to earn money. That's not right to do. I believe that you can get out of debt and improve your financial position by doing what you enjoy doing. **If you do what you love, you'll never work a day in your life.** Remember this quote. However, you cannot achieve that overnight. Until then you might need to do some jobs that you enjoy less. The second part of this chapter will be about finding a job that you can do (in order you are unemployed or you want to find another job and create another income source).

#1 - Find a job by spending no money.

1.   Get a full-time job – Finding a 9-5 job is what most people do. This is good because you earn guaranteed salary every month. A full time-job is a good stable income. It does take a third of your day, but hey, you still got two thirds available!

2.   Get a part-time job – The second option is getting a part-time job. You can get two part-time jobs and earn the same amount of money as a full-time job but be less bored instead. Now you have to consider the time you spend traveling.

3.   Fiverr – This website allows you to sell your skills. The main advantage of the website is that you can sell basically anything! ANYTHING! If you are good at history, math, science, a language, translation, writing, programming, editing, photography or anything at all, you can make money!

4.   Kindle – Amazon created an amazing platform where you can publish your books! If you are good at writing and you have something you want to write about, then you have to try this! You can take 35% - 70% royalty depends on the price of the book. I

recommend discussing your idea with someone who has knowledge in Internet Marketing because although the writing part is the most valuable part, you also need to know how to position your book, which keywords to use and how to market it during the free days. There are many strategies, but even with 0 knowledge you can still make money. The good part about this is that there is no limit about the number of books you can publish and you create a passive income source! You can write 10 books this year and you will get revenue from those books FOREVER!

5.   Udemy – This website allows you to create your own course and sell it to students. This is an amazing website designed for teachers. By teacher I do not mean someone who has a degree in a certain area and his profession is teaching people, but a person who has enough knowledge to teach others. There is a Facebook group made for all instructors so if you decide to create a course, they will answer all of your questions.

6.   Use Google/Yahoo/Bing or any other online search engine to find contests and competitions that you can apply to. The world has never been more globalized than it is today, and all that thanks to the internet.

7.   YouTube – Again, you need to find what you are good at and make videos about it. This belongs in the group of jobs that require no money start, but it requires a lot of knowledge about creating and editing the videos. However, if you are good at it, then you will do fine.

8.   oDesk / Elance – Using these two websites you can find jobs posted by employers and apply to them. I prefer oDesK as it is the best platform for this purpose. The advantage of being freelancer

is that you actually choose your own jobs! How good is that? But, the part that most people do not talk about is the competition. There are about 60.000 jobs opened and over 600.000 active freelancers. You can expect about 5-30 other applicants on the same job (depends on the job) and you need to think and understand what makes you different and better. You need to convince the person offering the job that you are the right person for the job and that you are better than the others.

9.   Spark Profit – A website and an application that allows you to earn money by predicting the price of Oil, copper, gold, S&P and foreign currencies. By guessing, you earn points that are converted to real money at the end of the week. You can earn up to $100 per month. This is something that you can do in your free time, when you are tired or bored. You can do it while waiting for the bus or during commercials. You don't have to invest anything at all! Also, there's a way to invite friends and they are registered as your supporters. This is important because you earn 10% of what they earn, not from their pocket, but from Spark Profit. If you are able to find 20 people that are really good at this, and each of them earns $40 per month, you get $4 per person! That's $80 per month and you are doing nothing at all. However, predicting the prices is not that easy, but it is definitely a good way to spend the time when you are bored or tired.

#2 - Find a job by spending money.

Obviously, the only way to find a job by spending money is to create yourself one. In order to create yourself a job with money, you need to start your own company. Most people in debt have ideas about creating their own business, but they are not sure if their idea is good or not. Well, you can find that out, but before you start, you have to make a short research about it. You cannot make a deep research unless you have knowledge about finance and accounting, but you can hire someone. However, if there is assumption that you are already in debt based on the fact that you are reading the book, then hiring someone and paying is not an option. If you want to create a research you can use the Internet. I am going to create a short list of what you need to do in order to find out if your idea is good or not.

1.   Analyze the market. If you want to open a store, take a look at all the stores in your city. Are they earning a lot of money or not? Now, obviously, the stores exists therefore they must have higher revenues than expenses. However, you have to have a criteria and make sure you are satisfied by the amount they earn. You can find out this very easy, either by contacting the owners or using the internet.

2.   Analyze the environment. If you are happy by the results that the stores are achieving, are you sure that you will have the same results in the environment you choose? Is there enough traffic around, are there enough people passing by, are there tourists passing by? Are there more or less people passing by compared to the other stores? Is it near the railway/bus station? These are questions that you can ask yourself.

3.   Analyze the competitors. Where they are buying the products? How much do they pay for them? Is there a way to reduce a cost that other stores have but are not aware of? Is there something you can change and make your store better than the competitors?

4.   Create your projected income statement. Put all the revenues on one side (Estimated sales in $ for a store) and all the

expenses on the other side (rent, utilities, insurance, costs of products you buy, salaries and so on). Make sure you don't miss an expense! Also, you need to be careful when you estimate your sales. You have to come up with a realistic or even pessimistic number based on FACTS! Not an imaginary number.

These are 4 basic steps that you can do on your own. Now, it might seem simple, but it's not. It takes a lot of time and at the end you might find out that your idea is not good enough and you will be disappointed.

However, if we assume that you have an amazing idea and you it is profitable according to your research, you have to move to step 2, that's creating the business plan. This is very hard to do on your own unless you have knowledge in this area. However, if you are not familiar with it, I recommend you hire someone with knowledge and experience creating business plans. You can use the business plan in order to get money.

Step 3 – Get money. It is simple as that. If you have an idea and a business plan, then all you need is money to start. There are two ways to get money:

1.   Get a loan. This is something that I recommend you NOT to do! If you are already in debt and you are not sure how to improve your financial position, DO NOT DO THIS! It is risky and you might end up with even higher debt than what you have right now.

2.   Find investor. This is what I recommend you do. You can make a deal and share the profit or maybe payback the amount in the next 10-15 years plus interest rate, if your business is successful. This might be hard, but with a good idea and well written business plan, it is not that hard.

Warren Buffett on earnings – "Never depend on a single income. Make investments to create a second source."

You must have in mind this quote by probably the best investors of all time, so do different jobs until you create a solid passive income.

#3 – Make money by investing

The 3rd way to make money is by investing. You're probably wondering why there is such chapter in this book. Why a person with debt would read about investment when he probably has no money. Well, what if a friend of yours wants to open a company and he tells you that he needs $2.000 and that if you borrow him this amount of money, he will pay you back with an interest of 12%. Let's imagine that he needs $4.000 in order to start the business and he got a loan of $2.000 from the bank. Now, if the bank offers you a loan with an interest rate of 6%, it means you can use this opportunity to make money. Of course, assuming that your friend's company will be successful. You will borrow $2.000 from the bank and you need to pay $2,000.00 * (1 + interest rate) = $2,000.00 * (1.06) = $2,120.00 at the end of the year. On the other hand, your friend has to pay you $2,000.00 * (1.12) = $2,240.00. You earn $120 by doing nothing at all. Now, I am not saying that this is something you have to do, but it is a way to earn money. If you consider that you have knowledge in investing, you can get a loan and invest in stocks. As long as the return of what you invest in is higher than the interest rate, you are doing good job.

How to calculate the return on a stock:

Stock return = Dividend yield + Capital gain

Dividend yield = amount of money received as dividend / price paid for the stock

Capital gain = (the current stock price – the price paid for the stock) / price paid for the stock

Example: Bill bought a common stock and paid $40. One year later, the price of the stock is $43 and Bill also received a dividend of $5 during the year.

Return Rate = 5/40 + (43-40)/40 = 0.2 = 20%

*If Bill took a loan at interest rate of 7% and invested them in the stock, he would've had a profit of the 13% difference. That's $5.2 (0.13 * $40).*

Saving and spending money

Now, as we mentioned, you get debt if you spend more money than you spend. If you earn more, it does not mean that you will improve your financial position. UNLESS, you spend less! You can even improve your financial position if you keep earning the same amount of money, but spending less. There are couple of rules that are really important when it comes to saving and also I am going to quote some famous people on their opinion about savings.

Rules:

1. If you want to buy something, make sure you pay the right price for it. It happened to me a couple of times to buy a product and then see the exactly same product a bit cheaper somewhere else. I cannot blame anyone else, but me. If you want to buy something, don't rush. Take your time, check different stores, search online, and then make the right decision.

2. Don't buy something you don't need. There's a quote that says "We buy things we don't need with money we don't have to impress people we don't like." And this is very true, especially to people that are in debt. I am not going to go in details how a person gets his/her debt because that's not the purpose of this book. So, before you buy something, make sure it is something you need.

These are two very, very important rules! If you are able to think rationally, you will be able to control the way you spend your money.

We are going to focus on the 1st one as the 2nd one is self-explanatory. People are getting used to what they do and create routines. They buy bread from the same store, beer from the same store, meat from the same store and so on. I am not saying that this is wrong. However, this has influence on your financial position. I realized that when I was buying bread. The difference of the price of the bread between two stores was $0.4. Yes, it is not a lot. But my family was consuming 2 breads every day. So, if we buy the cheaper one, we are going to save $0.8 per day or $292 per year! You might say that it is not a lot. It is true, but this is only one product! Imagine everything that you buy! Before you buy a product, research not only in the stores in your neighbor or city, but online as-well (depends on the product of course). If you want to buy clothes or shoes than you can easily find discounts online so it is worth wasting couple of minutes researching.

Your Balance Sheet

Until now, you read what debt is, and how to get out of debt (by earning more and spending less). You might've known a lot of what was written until now. This chapter and the next one will help you to understand how you can create your own secret formula.

A balance sheet is a document that all companies have, regardless of their size. It shows all the assets they have, all the liabilities and the equity. It is called balance because it has an equation called *the accounting equation* and it is always in balance. The accounting equation is **Asset = Liabilities + Equity**

I will not go into details in this. However, I am going to say couple of words about each of this.

Assets are things that the company owns. Money, land, equipment, cars and so on.

Liabilities are sums of money that the company owes.

Equity is the difference between the assets and the liabilities (If we put liabilities on the other side of the equation, we get Assets – Liabilities = Equity) and sometimes it is a good indicator for the company.

Anyway, I am going to modify this equation and make it suitable for you.

In order to understand your financial position, you need to know all of the assets and liabilities you have. However, according to the accounting equation, you can have more assets than liabilities and still be in a bad financial position. Example, if you have a car that's worth $20.000 and you owe $3.000, you won't be really happy about it, because in order to pay the debt, you have to sell your house. So, as I said earlier, I am going to not only modify the formula, but change the definition of assets. If you want to find out your financial position, create a list of all the assets you have, but don't add those assets that you can afford to sell (car, house, land, equipment and so on). So basically, make a list of cash and cash equivalents that you have. The second list that you need to make is the list of the liabilities. Make a list of all the liabilities that you have regardless of the time you have to pay them. You can do it on a piece of paper or in Excel. It is very simple and easy to do.

Why create a list? I already know that I have debt.

This is probably what you're wondering right now. Why create a list? Well, when you have everything written and you are aware of it, it has bigger influence on your life and you will pay more attention to it. This is very important and it will become clearer in the next chapter where you will read about goals.

Once you have the list, you can see the amount of money you need in order to break-even. You know the sum of money you need in order to pay all of your liabilities and be in a position with assets and liabilities that have value of $0.

Personal Balance Sheet

By filling out a personal balance sheet, you will be able to determine your net worth. Finding out your net worth is an important early step in the process of becoming a business owner because you need to find out what assets are available to you for investment in your business.

Statement of Financial Condition _____ 20____

Assets		TOTALS	
Cash/Checking and Savings Accounts			
Marketable Securities			
Nonmarketable Securities			
Real Estate/Home			
Partial Interest in Real Estate			
Automobiles			
Personal Property			
Personal Loans			
Insurance Cash Values			
Other			
Total Assets	A		

Liabilities		TOTALS	
Secured Loans			
Unsecured Loans			
Credit Card/Charge Account Bills			
Personal Debts			
Current Monthly Bills			
Real Estate Mortgages			
Unpaid Income Tax			
Other Unpaid Taxes and Interest			
Other Itemized Debts			
Total Liabilities	B		
Net Worth (A − B = C)	C		
Total Liabilities & Net Worth	D		

Degree of Debt
Note:
If total liabilities exceed total assets, subtract assets from liabilities to determine degree of debt (B − A = E)

Total Liabilities	B	
Total Assets	A	
Degree of Debt	E	

Find more forms for your business at www.entrepreneur.com/formnet.

Find more forms for your business at www.entrepreneur.com/formnet.

Schedule and goals

Until now, you are familiar with what debt is, different ways of earning money, how to spend/save money and you know your financial position. The only thing that's left is to improve your financial position, something that you are hoping to learn throughout this book and you are finally here! In the 1st part I said that there is no secret formula that works for everyone. You need to create your own based on your skills, your knowledge and your experience.

A very important rule – Do not depend on a single income. I mentioned this before and I will do it again. This is very important! You have to find a way to create as many incomes as possible.

Step 1 – Choose how you are going to make money. You can have a part-time job, then writing books at your free time, applying for jobs on oDesk or something as simple as playing Spark Profit https://sparkprofit.com/ while you wait for the bus.

Step 2 – See how well you are managing your expenses. Make sure you buy the products at the best price for you.

Step 3 – **SET GOALS** – The reasons this is bolded is because it is something that is new in the book. Earlier in the book you read about creating a list of all your liquid assets and liabilities and that you know the amount of money you need in order to break-even. That could be your first goal. However, you should also set a deadline. You need to manage your time. If you do all of this you will improve your financial position really quick. You should have a lot of small goals that lean towards your main goal – **getting out of debt and improving your financial position**.

Examples of goals:

1. Write 1.000 words per day – If you decide to write books.

2.   Create 2 minutes video – If you decide to create videos for Udemy or YouTube.

3.   Create 2 gigs – If you decide to sell fiver gigs.

4.   Find cheaper products – In order to save money when spending money.

5.   Find good stocks to invest in – If you decide to invest in the stock market.

Now, it is very important to have goals **every day.** You can have daily goals, like the ones mentioned above, but you can also have **monthly goals** and even **yearly goals**. You can write your daily goals at the end of the day and read them in the morning. You can revise and edit anytime, but try to stick to what you wrote at the first place. Don't be afraid and move back. If you do this every day for at least 3 weeks, your brain will get used to it.

Now you know more than enough to create your own schedule and plan to get out of debt and improve your financial position. Create the right formula for you and start living a better life!

In this short book you read enough information and practical examples about what debt is, how to earn money, how to spend and save money and how to set your own goals.

You are ready to take care of your life. You are ready to take your financial future in your hands and shape it the way you want it to look.

All you need to do is follow the advices given in this short book and not give up. And remember, if someone can do it, you can do it as-well. There are plenty of people that were in debt, but they are doing fine now. You can do it too.

Good luck!

Author Bio

Author Name: Kostadin Ristovski

Since he was a young boy, he had eye for details and he was very passionate about it. Kostadin was born in small town near Pearland, Texas.

After finishing high school, he was not sure which road to take between accounting, MBA and Financial Management. He decided to go for MBA, however, he kept learning about many other things in his free time.

He was also the captain of the basketball club and he was very good at it. He led the team on couple of times when the coach was sick and he was doing really good job at it.

After finishing college, he had 6 different jobs as intern as he wanted to learn as much as possible about the culture in different companies.

In the past 20 years, he is the manager of his own company where he works as consultant. He is married and has 3 children.

Check out some of the other JD-Biz Publishing books

Gardening Series on Amazon

Country Life Books

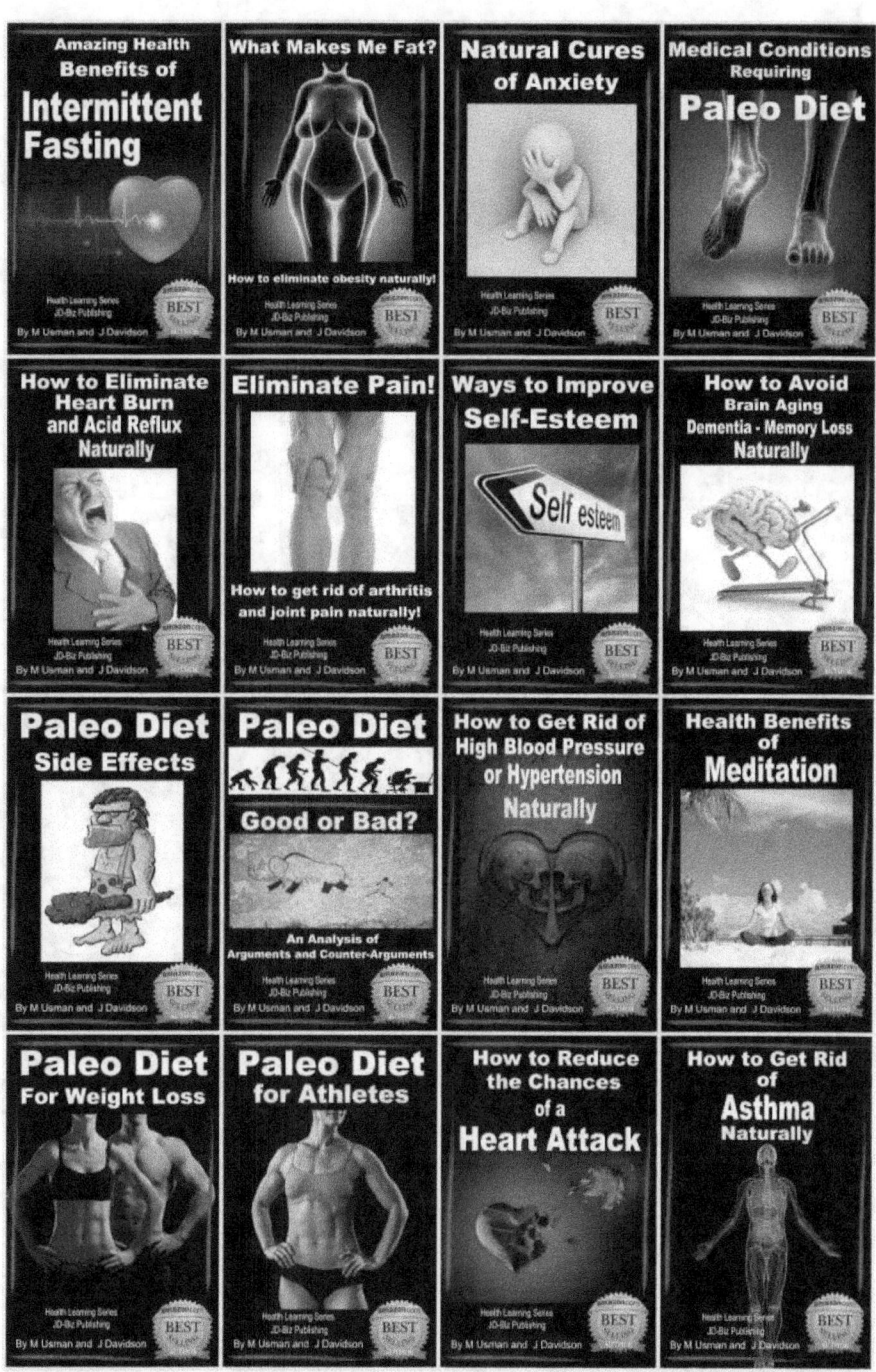

Learn To Draw Series

How to Build and Plan Books

Entrepreneur Book Series

Our books are available at

1. Amazon.com

2. Barnes and Noble

3. Itunes

4. Kobo

5. Smashwords

6. Google Play Books

Publisher

JD-Biz Corp

P O Box 374

Mendon, Utah 84325

http://www.jd-biz.com/

Mendon Cottage Books

P O Box 374, Mendon Utah 84325